People and Birds are Exactly Alike Except for the Feathers

Without the feathers, you can hardly tell them apart!

What Kind of Bird Are You?

Story line Graphic Design: **John Kaufman**

People and Birds are Exactly Alike Except for the Feathers

Copyright © 2024 by John Kaufman. All rights reserved.

No part of this publication may be reproduced, distributed, or transmitted in any form or by any means, including photocopying, recording, or other electronic or mechanical methods, without the prior written permission of the author, except in the case of brief quotations embodied in critical reviews and certain other noncommercial uses permitted by copyright law.

The contents of this work, including, but not limited to, the accuracy of events, people, and places depicted; opinions expressed; permission to use previously published materials included; and any advice given or actions advocated are solely the responsibility of the author, who assumes all liability for said work and indemnifies the publisher against any claims stemming from publication of the work.

Printed in the United States of America
ISBN 978-1-64133-962-9 (sc)
ISBN 978-1-64133-963-6 (e)
ISBN 978-1-64133-961-2 (hc)

This book is printed on acid-free paper.

Because of the dynamic nature of the Internet, any web addresses or links contained in this book may have changed since publication and may no longer be valid. The views expressed in this work are solely those of the author and do not necessarily reflect the views of the publisher, and the publisher hereby disclaims any responsibility for them.

2024.11.21

Blue Ink Media Solutions
1111B S Governors Ave
STE 7582 Dover,
DE 19904

www.blueinkmediasolutions.com

What Kind of Bird Are You?

Birds and people are very much alike;
without their feathers, you can hardly tell them apart.

There are a few exceptions to the rule.
We know, birds would never wear clothes; however, people have been dressing up in feathers soon
after they captured their first bird.

It has been said that,
"A Bird in the hand is worth three in the bush!"

Not only were the feathers beautiful, but they also made pretty things to wear—the feathers worn by those that loved the feathers more than they did the birds. There are a lot of birds, and everyone is a different color. What color are the feathers you like to wear?

 What kind of bird are you?

We love our cats and they love to chase, catch and eat our feathery birds.

First, look around you. Do you have a family?
Do you have brothers and sisters?

Most birds have a mom and a dad. How many people do you have in your families nest?

Where will I find you, living in a bush, a house built in a city, or a forest full of trees? Where will I see you, on the ground, in the sky, or living in a tree?

"No one is free; even the birds are chained to the sky."
Bob Dylan

Perhaps you live on the water. Many birds do!

Other birds like the owl prefer to live in dry places, like in a hollow tree where others can't see them while they sleep.

Where ever you choose to live. I hope it's safe,
not too hot and not too frosty cream cold!

The morning dove makes her nest of a few broken sticks, and there she raises her brood, while others would never live in such an awful place, regardless of the view!

"Birds teach us something very important: You will finally come down to the ground to whatever height you rise."

Mehmet Murat Ildan

I am the kind of bird that likes to travel from here to there.

I spent my summers in the east and my winters in the south.

Most times, I am either her or there or somewhere in between.

I am a bird that likes to live alone,
as birds and people sometimes do.
It can be a lonely life if you are a solitary
bird while other birds, like people,
choose to find mate for life.

When we are young and can't walk or fly,
we stay in the place our parents decide.

  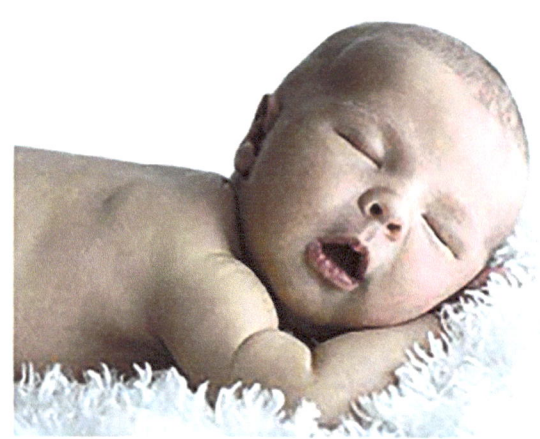

One day soon, before too long, you'll be all grown
up and learn to run, dance, and know how to fly.

You will be old enough to find a nest in a lovely house of your own.

Every house is different, and every place is someone's home! Where would you build your nest? Where would you call home?

While other birds look different, not like you or me, the colors in our feathers are the way nature thought they should be!

"Flying may not be all plain sailing, but the fun of it is worth the price!"

Amelia Earheart

If I were a bird, I would have some pretty feathers on top of my head that made me feel real proud,' and when I hung around other birds like me, we make a good-looking crowd.

"Always build a nest in a very tall tree, where a big hand cannot reach you!"

Old bird in the bush Proverb

Some birds are very selfish!
Some are bigger, faster,
mush quicker, far smarter too.
While those birds are smaller,
can't find enough food to eat, it's true.

Birds like People, eat many things.
Seeds, berries, wheat and oats.
People like birds they love to eat, a berry
down in each birdie's throat.

"A Bird in the hand is worth two in the bush!"
Old pheasant hunter proverb

Many kinds of birds, like some people look alike when perched in the edge!

"Use the talents you process: The woods would be very silent if no birds sang there except those that sang best."

Henry Van Dyke

Some birds, like people, have long legs.
They can run extremely fast,
standing up very tall.
With their wings, they can soar above those
below, who only walk, run, or crawl!

Some friends of mine want to stay up
all night and play peak-ka-Boo.

I prefer to be with birds that love to sing, dance, and cuddle.
Just before my eyes I find my friend so we can snuggle!

Not me. I am a curious bird, a comfy nest, and an excellent book to read, and that's the kind of bird I am.

What kind of bird are you?

The sound of birds stops
"the noise in my head."
Carly Simon

Legs that turn out long or short are always meant to be! Birds have legs and two feet, so they can scratch in the dirt for something good to eat!

"You cannot fly like an eagle with the wings of a wren!"
William Henry Hudson

Every person, bird, and animal I have ever met was different, with different personalities. Like so many people you always remember, and others you soon forget.

People and birds are very much alike except for the feathers.

Some birds seem pretty happy, while other birds seem quite sad. Some birds are just like some people, always up to something not good but bad!

People sometimes are said to have a bird's brain. All kidding aside, most birds, like most people, are really smart.

If your parents are love birds, then you might be a love bird too. If you were a bird, what kind of *bird* would you be? Would you live in a big house or in a nest inside a big oak tree?

Look around you, and you will find birds of a feather stick together.

Some birds are intelligent, and you can teach them to talk, dance, and sing. They can play musical instruments and do unbelievable things.

While, unlike birds, many people like to only watch television and never learn to sing and dance. What kind of bird are you?

Some birds are very brilliant, while others are not so bright. Still their beauty is here for all of us to bird watch morning, noon, or night!

When you're a bird, you can fly from here to there, because birds with wings can fly anywhere.

The eagle soars up to the sky where planes and astronauts fly. I'm the bird that likes to fly, but not too fast and certainly not too high.

Some birds cannot fly, so they use their legs to get where they want to go. Some are fast, and some are very slow.

Depending on what kind of bird you are,
that is where I will find you.

I'm the kind of bird who likes to have a family and kind loving friends. What kind of bird are you?

"You cannot fly like an eagle with wings of a dove!"
William Henry

I'm the kind of bird that does not prefer a nest in a wire home.

I would instead remain carefree and have the world to Rome!

"God loved the birds and invented the trees.
Man loved the birds and invented the birdcage."
Jacques Deval

"No bird soars too high if he soars with his own wings!"
William Blake

How do you walk, and how do you talk?
What kind of bird are you?
The person you are and the person
you become tell us other birds,
what kind of bird you are!

"Never peck on others today,
as you will get pecked on much worst tomorrow!"

Old chicken Proverb

What kind of bird are you? Happy, Sad, Talkative, Lazy? Lonely, Silly, Fun, Confident, Ordinary, Hungry, Big, Small, Cry-birdie, Lovable, Talented, Quiet, loud? Are you a Boy or Girl?

No matter what the colors in the feathers that you wear, fluff your feathers up and watch people stare!

The End

www.ingramcontent.com/pod-product-compliance
Lightning Source LLC
Chambersburg PA
CBHW041644070526

44585CB00004B/125